THE BR
HORSE S(

GW00420330

THE RIDGEWAY DOW

AVAILABLE IN THIS SERIES

First published 1994
by The British Horse Society
Access & Rights of Way Department
British Equestrian Centre
Stoneleigh Park, Kenilworth
Warwickshire CV8 2LR

A catalogue record for this book is available from the British Library

ISBN 1 899016 03 1

Printed by:
Tripod Press Limited, 7 Wise Street, Leamington Spa, CV31 3AP

Distribution: The British Horse Society, Stoneleigh Park, Kenilworth,
Warwickshire, CV8 2LR

CONTENTS

ACKNOWLEDGEMENTS

The British Horse Society would like to thank Penny Reid, Janice Bridger, Hazel Smith, Charlotte Swann, John Winkley and Tim Moore for surveying, developing and describing the sixteen trails contained in this guide book.

They have chosen what many would describe as the finest off-road riding in England.

Financial assistance from Berkshire County Council and general support through their rights of way staff was essential to the successful completion of this important riding network and the British Horse Society extends to them, a sincere vote of thanks.

FOREWORD

The '................ on Horseback' series of published rides launched in 1993 has proved extremely popular. This confirms the British Horse Society's belief that many riders need information on routes known to be open, available and providing pleasurable riding.

Many volunteers have worked to research these routes, thus helping to contribute to the Countryside Commission's target of having all rights of way defined, open and signed by the year 2000. This Society wholeheartedly supports this aim which it incorporates into its Access & Rights of Way strategy for the last decade of this Century.

Together with our booklet 'Bed & Breakfast for Horses', these publications enable riders and carriage drivers to plan holidays and other trips. This extends the pleasure and value of owning a horse either to ride or drive, and enables an assortment of different experiences to be enjoyed be they landscape, flora and fauna or historic sites and buildings.

Equestrianism provides one of the most intense pleasures of life, wholly understood only by those who ride, or drive carriages. The Society is proud to contribute in some way to the fulfilment of that pleasure. The challenges of research and development of further routes will continue to be explored.

E A T BONNOR-MAURICE
Chairman, British Horse Society

March 1994

INTRODUCTION

The British Horse Society's ARROW Project aims to identify open and usable routes of varying length and shape (circular, figure-of-eight or linear) to help riders and carriage drivers to enjoy the countryside by means, as far as possible, of the network of public rights of way and the minor vehicular highways. This collection of rides is the result of research and mapping by volunteers who took up the challenge of the ARROW initiative with such enthusiasm and effort.

I am faced with the equally daunting challenge of writing an introductory chapter. Should I write reams about each topic or try simply to point you in the right direction? I have decided upon the second method as the search for information is itself highly educative and stays in the mind better than reading it all in one place. Also, since we all have different expectations of our holiday, a very full guide seemed wrong. Nevertheless, there are a few pointers I would like to suggest to you.

The most important one is to start your planning several months in advance of the trip, including a visit to the area you intend to ride in. You should make endless lists of things to DO (e.g. get the saddle checked) and things to CHECK OUT (can you read a map, for instance). You may find joining the local BHS Endurance Riding Group very helpful, as there you will meet people who can give you information about the degree of fitness needed for yourself and your horse (feeding for fitness not dottiness) , and many other useful hints on adventurous riding. You may also enjoy some of the Pleasure rides organised by the group or by the local Riding Club. These are usually about 15-20 miles and you ride in company,

though using a map. You may find them under the title Training Rides. These rides will get both of you used to going into strange country. If you usually ride on well-known tracks, then your horse will find it nerve-racking to go off into new territory, and you yourself may also find the excitement of deep country a bit surprising, so try to widen your experience at home before you go off on holiday.

ACCOMMODATION

Decide how far you wish to ride each day of your holiday, book overnight accommodation for both of you and if possible visit it to see if the five-star suite on offer to your horse is what he is used to. Decide if you want to stable him or to turn him out at the end of the day, and arrange to drop off some food for him, as he will not relish hard work on a diet of green grass, nor will he enjoy a change in his usual food. If you are to have a back-up vehicle, of course, then you will not need to do some of this, but you should certainly make a preliminary visit if you can. The BHS publish a Bed & Breakfast Guide for Horses which is a list of people willing to accommodate horses, and sometimes riders, overnight. The Society does not inspect these places, so you should check everything in advance.

FITNESS

You and your horse should be fit. For both of you , this is a process taking about two months. If you and/or your horse are not in the full flush of youth, then it may take a bit longer. The office chair, the factory floor, or the household duties do not make or keep you fit, but carefully planned exercise will. Remember that no matter how fit your horse seems, he does not keep himself fit - you get him fit. There are several books with details of fitness programmes for a series of rides. Do not forget to build in a rest day during your holiday - neither of you can keep going all the time, day after day. Miles of walking may get you fit, but it uses different muscles from riding; you may get a surprise when you start riding longer distances. It seems to me that the further you intend to ride, the longer your preparation should be. Nothing can be done in a hurry.

Your horse should be obedient, so work on that. If you want him to stand, then he must stand. If you want to go through water, then he must be prepared to walk down a slope or even step down off a bank to go through the stream, so start with puddles and insist that he go through the middle. Does he help you open gates? I hope so, or you will have a great deal of mounting and dismounting to do. Does he tie up - this is essential if you are to have a peaceful pint at lunchtime.

MAPS

Can you read a map? Can you make and read a grid reference (usually referred to as GR)? Get a Pathfinder map of your area and take yourself for a walk and see if you end up where you expect to. Learn to know exactly where you are on the map, and how to understand the symbols (if your map shows hilly ground, the journey will take longer). Can you work out how long a ride is in miles and roughly how long it will take? You will be using rights of way and it is very important that you stay in the line of the path - that is the only place you have a right to be, and you may deviate from that line only as much as is necessary to get you round an obstruction on the path. You are going to be riding over land that forms part of someone's work place

and that fact must be respected. It is only by the efforts of farmers and landowners that the countryside exists in its present form - so that we may enjoy it as we pass by.

You will need to know the grid reference (GR.) of the start and end of the various tracks you are to use. Get a copy of an Ordnance Survey (OS) Landranger map and really learn the details on the right-hand side, some of which explain how to arrive at a Grid Reference. Learn to go in the door (Eastings - from left to right) and up the stairs (Northings - from bottom to top). There is a great deal of information on the Landranger maps and not so much on the Pathfinders, but the Pathfinder gives more details on the map itself, so that is the map you will use for the actual ride. Or you may care to buy a Landranger of the area you are visiting and, using a highlighter pen, mark in all the rides you want to make, so that you can see through the marks you make. Then get from any Outdoor shop a map case which will allow you to read the map without taking it out of the case and which you can secure round yourself. Also, you should know if you are facing north, south, east or west as you ride. Quite important if you think about it, as it is no good riding into the sunset if you are meant to be going south. Plastic orienteering compasses are cheap and reliable.

TACK

Have your tack thoroughly checked by your saddler, as there is nothing so annoying as a sore back which could have been prevented, or an unnecessarily broken girth strap. How are you going to carry the essential headcollar and rope each day? What about spare shoes, or a false shoe?

What to take on the ride depends on how much back-up you have. If you have to carry a change of clothes, etc., then you are into very careful planning indeed - balance saddle bag, the lot. If you are based at your first night stop all the time, then life is much easier. You should always carry a first aid kit for horse and rider. You will also have to plan how to wash the girth and numnah. Remember our delightful climate and always carry a waterproof and additional warm clothing - it never pays to gamble with rain and wind.

SAFETY

It is always wiser to ride in company. The other person can always hold your horse, or pull you out of the ditch, as well as being someone to talk to about the excitements of the day and to help plan everything. You should always wear a BSI riding hat, properly secured, and also safe footwear. You need a clearly defined heel and a smooth sole. Even if riding in company, tell someone where you are going and roughly how long you expect to take. If affordable, take a portable telephone. Make a list of the things you must carry every day and check it before leaving base.

INSURANCE

You should have Third Party Legal Liability Insurance. This will protect you if you or your horse cause a bit of mayhem (accidentally!). Membership of the BHS gives you this type of insurance, plus Personal Accident Insurance as part of the membership package. Check your household insurance to make sure it covers riding before you rely only on that, as some insurances do not. You should always have this type of cover when venturing forth into the outside world, even if it is an hours hack from home.

PARKING

If you intend to box to the start of the day's ride, either have someone to take the box away or make sure it is safely, securely and considerately parked. If you have to make arrangements to park, do it well in advance or the contact may well have gone to market or the hairdressers when you make a last minute call. Have the vehicle number etched on to the windows for security.

MONEY

This is vital, so work out a system of getting money if necessary. Sadly we can no longer gallop up to the bank and lead Dobbin into the cashier's queue, nor do most banks have hitching rails. Post Offices are more numerous and might be a useful alternative. Always have the price of a telephone call on you.

Lastly, if you do run into problems of blocked paths or boggy ones, write to the Highway Authority of the relevant county council and tell them. Then you can do something about it. You might even think of adopting a path near home and keeping an eye on it, telling your own county council of any difficulties you encounter. It is through such voluntary work that these rides have been made possible.

Wherever you ride, always do it responsibly, with care of the land, consideration for the farmer and courtesy for all other users. Remember the Country Code and enjoy your ARROW Riding.

I hope this chapter will have started you planning and making lists. If I seem to be always writing about forward planning it is only because I usually leave things to the last minute, which causes chaos!

PHILIPPA LUARD

THE RIDGEWAY DOWNS

It may be that the writer is biased but a study of the Pathfinder's Ordnance Survey Map for Wantage (South) and Didcot (East) does make one feel that there can be few areas in Great Britain where the ancient and the very modern are in such close and contrasting proximity.

Within GR 40 and 48 and GR 85 and 90 there lies a Bronze Age thoroughfare (The Great Ridgeway), a medieval village (East Hendred), an Atomic Research Establishment (Harwell), a Roman Road (The Icknield Way), a legendary battle site - King Alfred's conflict at Wantage.

But the backdrop to all this, is the great panorama of the Ridgeway Downs. From the riders' point of view, the Ridgeway does indeed extend from Avebury to Pangbourne but for the purposes of this booklet we are dealing with the western section north of the M4 from Foxhill (the Shepherd's Rest Public House) to Compton and Blewbury. The amazing thing about this area, which includes Wiltshire, Oxfordshire and Berkshire, is that it is simply crammed with Rights of Way, bridlepaths and byways the majority of which have no gates and are pleasant and easy to ride along. Indeed any Endurance Rider of a few years' experience can testify to the fact that the two day Wantage Ride held in May setting out from Lockinge just outside this attractive market town with a statue of the cake-burning monarch at its centre, is perhaps of all rides held in England at least, the one with the fewest gates to open. The chalky soil is well drained and for the most part the Rights of Way are wide and dry; the Ridgeway itself has had a great deal of work done to improve the going on this track which is to some extent the 'M4' or 'M1' of British Rights of Way, so popular is it with walkers and mountain bikers.

As far as numbers of riders are concerned however, there are comparatively few leisure riders to be seen from Fox Hill to Compton as the Ridgeway Downs are dominated by thoroughbreds in training. Every sort of racehorse is worked upon these great grassy stretches, from fragile two year olds with legs like glass and eyes on stalks to tough old 'chasers, wise-headed and lean. Rather like Cinderella's Ball, though, all these racehorses disappear as if by magic at the stroke of twelve - midday - almost without exception, leaving the Downs to the skylarks and partridges and hares. It is easy then, to ride for hours without seeing another horse or human.

Perhaps one should mention at this point that although the marked stretches of the gallops do represent great temptations for anyone with a fit horse in need of a 'pipe-opener', they are privately owned and maintained at great expense - so hooves off!

As I indicated at the start, this area is above all rich in history. Recent archaeological research done during the summer of 1993 in the immediate vicinity of the White Horse of Uffington has revealed that this famous chalk hill figure formed part of a great prehistoric funerary complex, used for more than

4000 years, from about 3500 BC. Facing the horse's head, archaeologists have found the remains of a 25 metre long, 5500 year old burial mound together with evidence that 80 to 100 third to fourth century AD Romano-Britons were also buried there.

All kinds of other tombs from the Bronze Age to Anglo-Saxon times were discovered just above the horse's head which suggests that throughout these times some sort of ritual activity was carried on.

The horse itself was probably carved in the Iron Age - a period in which the dead were seldom buried, their remains being disposed of in other yet undetermined ways. This probably explains the absence of any burials around the horse dating from the Iron Age - the 800 year period from the end of the Bronze Age to the first century AD Roman Conquest.

The archeologists feel that the chalk carving reflects the importance of the horse in religion and ritual in these early times. Throughout Celtic Europe horses were high status animals and indeed were deified in the shape of Epona, the Celtic horse goddess and her British equivalent Rhiannon. Both deities were protectors of the dead and also viewed as mother goddesses responsible for fertility.

As was very usual, with the coming of Christianity, the site was brought into that religion and the horse was changed into St George's charger and the hill side deemed to be the very place where the dragon was slain. Clearly, however, such a metamorphosis was only a very light veneer of Christianization for a site with deep roots of pagan belief and ritual.

Today the worship of the horse continues as the 'strings' nod and float around these Downs, the hopes and fortunes of owners, trainers and stable lads and lasses following them ceaselessly. We, the leisure riders, can only wonder at the logic of it all and admire the four-legged athletes and their dedicated minders.

BRIDLEWAYS

HOW TO FIND YOURS

There are many miles of rights of way throughout the country on which you may ride: these fall into three types: they are Bridleways, Byways Open to All Traffic and Unclassified County Roads (which may be referred to as field roads or green lanes).

MAPS

The best maps to use while riding are the Ordnance Survey 1:25,000 (2.5" to the mile) Maps since these show the field boundaries. The maps of this scale, known as the Pathfinder Series, show Bridleways as a line of green dashes.

The Rights of Way information shown on a printed map was correct at the time that the map was printed but changes do take place: if you have any reason to query the Rights of Way information on a printed map it will be necessary for you to consult the Definitive Map and the County Council Rights of Way Officer to resolve the query.

The Definitive Map is a legal document held and maintained by the County Council; copies may also be found at County Council Area/Local/Divisional Offices and Parish Clerks'Offices and local libraries. The Definitive Maps are available for inspection by any member of public who wishes to see them. It would be a courtesy to telephone and ask for the relevant sheets to be made available.

THE BRITISH
HORSE SOCIETY

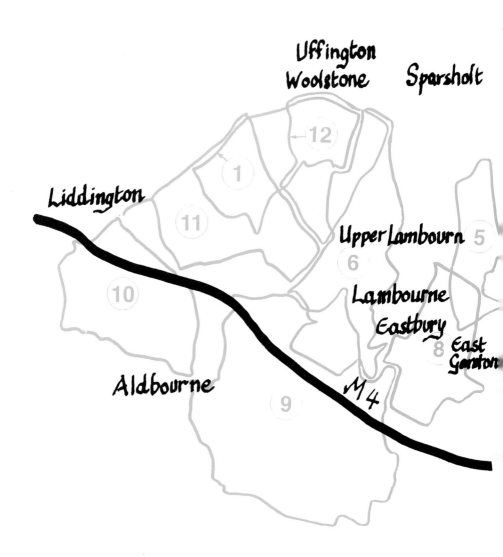

Uffington
Woolstone   Sparsholt

12

1

Liddington

11

Upper Lambourn   5

6

10

Lambourne

Eastbury

8   East
Garston

Aldbourne

M4

9

RIDGEWAY DOWNS
ON HORSEBACK

Vantage

14

Blewbury
3

15
West
Isley

2

Farnborough

13

South
Fawley

Brightwalton

7

East
Isley

Compton

4

Aldworth

Chaddleworth

Beedon

Great
Shefford

Leckhampstead

Hampstead
Norrey

Welford

M4

16

Newbury

WHITE HORSE HILL/ WAYLANDS SMITHY

A 12 MILE CIRCULAR TRAIL (ANTI-CLOCKWISE)

Ordnance Survey Maps:
Landranger: 174
Pathfinder: 1154

Parking & Starting Point:
Parking is available in the car park at Sparsholt Firs which is 4 miles north of Lambourn on the B4001 (GR.343851). The radio mast is a good landmark.

Of Interest:
The first part of the route follows The Ridgeway National Trail which is thought to be the oldest track in Europe. It runs along the high chalk downland from near Avebury in Wiltshire to Ivinghoe Beacon in Buckinghamshire. The Prehistoric people who were the first to use this track kept to the high ground for safety and because the light chalky soils were easier to clear and remained drier especially in winter. You will pass many signs of their presence - Stone Age long and round barrows, Iron Age forts and one of the finest of all prehistoric monuments - The Uffington White Horse which is believed to date from the late Iron Age (approximately 2000 years old).

Route Description:

1.   From your parking place, follow the Ridgeway westwards for 1.50 miles until you cross the Kingston Lisle to Lambourn road. Ride straight on to Whitehorse Hill - *The White Horse is on the slopes below Uffington Castle.* Continue for another 1.50 miles passing Waylands Smithy on your right - *a Stone Age long barrow signifying a*

ceremonial burial site dating from around 3000 BC containing communal burial chambers. It has been connected with later legends about Wayland the Smith (A Saxon god), who it is said, would shoe a horse if money was left on the top stone and the traveller did not return until the shoeing was over.

TRAIL 1.

2.   Continue on across the Ashbury to Lambourn road (B4000) to a group of buildings at a crossroads in the tracks (GR.264835). Take a track to the left, passing a barn on your left, and ride over Swinley Down, towards Ashdown Park - *the house was built in the 17th Century by the first Lord Craven as a hunting lodge. There is a large painting in the Tate Gallery showing foxhunting and coursing in a landscape and park that have hardly changed in three Centuries. The estate is now owned by The National Trust. The Park is open to the public all year round (Saturdays-Thursdays inclusive) and the house is open from April to October (Wednesdays and Saturdays).*

3.   Ride down the track past the main gates to the B4000. Turn right on to this road and continue until you reach the second bridleway on the left which is a wide chalky path. Follow this permitted bridleway up Weathercock Hill and then ride down steeply, alongside a fence line to a crossroads in the tracks (GR.298827). Continue straight on and then bear left following the fence line close to a small copse known as Knighton Bushes. The route now climbs steeply again up Whit Coombe Hill. At the top of the hill turn right then shortly after, go left and ride down alongside an all-weather gallop. *Below to your right is the Seven Barrows, another ancient monument - perhaps the finest example of Bronze Age burial mounds in the country - and the nearby training stables.*

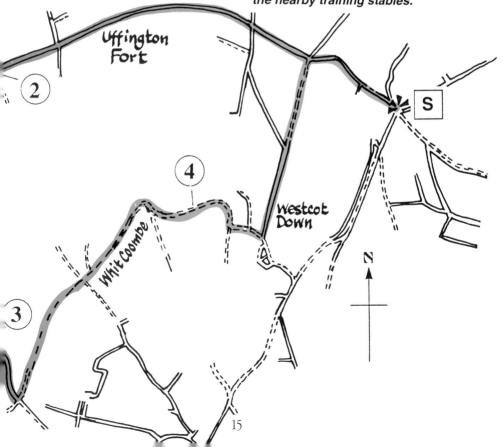

15

4. The bridleway bends to the right, then branches left to join the quiet road at Westcot Down. Turn left on to the road and then take the right fork along the track going straight back up to the Ridgeway. At the crossroads of tracks, turn right and so back to the car park at Sparsholt Firs.

NB: In summer time, downlands routes can be hot and particularly dry and water is sometimes difficult to find - you are advised to carry supplies with you although there is a water tap just to the west of the car park, beyond Hill Barn. There are also Public Houses not far off the Ridgeway at Woolstone and Kingstone Lisle, where it would be possible to get water.

Ashdown House

16

ISLEY DOWNS

TRAIL 2

A 15 MILE CIRCULAR TRAIL (CLOCKWISE)

Ordnance Survey Maps:
Landranger: 174
Pathfinder: 1171 & 1155

Parking & Starting Point:
Parking is available at Bury Down Car Park which lies north of West Ilsley, on the road from West Ilsley to Chilton (GR.479840).

Of Interest:
The Ilsley Downs Riding Route takes the rider along traffic-free lanes through the beautiful open and wooded countryside of the Berkshire Downs with its expansive views of the surrounding area. The route follows byways, bridleways and roads used as public paths and each change in direction is carefully signed with an arrow bearing the Ridgeway Downs Riding Route logo. The Ridgeway, one of the most ancient tracks in Europe, dates back to prehistoric times and is surrounded by the remains of earlier civilisations in the form of tumuli (Bronze Age round barrows), Stone Age long barrows and Iron Age forts.

On your way along The Ridgeway you may notice the remains of Grim's Ditch to the north, an important landholding division which once ran 24 miles to the River Thames, but which is now only evident in isolated stretches. At Cuckhamsley Hill the open vistas of downland are temporarily obscured by a small stand of trees which surround 'Scutchamer Knob', a barrow which is believed to be the burial place of King Cwicchelm of Wessex, who died in AD 593. The downland over which much of the route runs is chalk upland

which has a shallow soil profile. In the past this has proved unsuitable for ploughing and was left to be grazed by sheep, but with modern farming techniques it has been possible to turn the majority of this land over to crops.

The A34 is the main through-route between Southampton and the North West of Engalnd and at Gore Hill follows a similar line to that of the dismantled railway that used to link Oxford with Newbury and Southampton.

East Ilsley is an attractive village containing a 13th Century church. Typically plain in design, the church contains a brass (1606) to Katharine Hildeslea, the surname being that from which 'Ilsley' is derived. East Ilsley, like Lambourn further to the west, is now best known as a centre for racehorse training, relying as it does on the lush, springy turf which carpets the Downs encircling the village. In former times, most notably in the Middle Ages, the village was an important centre specialising in the sheep trade. It was not unknown for several thousand sheep and lambs to be auctioned within a single day, the beasts having been driven down the narrow roads and tacks that lead into the village. Old Street Lane, as the name suggests, is an ancient track which ran from the south of Newbury (Walbury Hill) to the Seven Barrows.

You may wish to visit West Ilsley by taking one of the signposted rights of way off the Ridgeway. Although traditionally of less significance than its eastern neighbour, the village has an unusual history. Perhaps

17

the most notable event relates to one of the former custodians of the church, an Archbishop of Spalato (Split) who journeyed to England following profound disagreements with the Pope in 1616. On his arrival he became a Protestant, subsequently rector of the parish and later Dean of Windsor. Eventually he returned to Rome mistakenly believing he would be made Cardinal, however the unfortunate man was imprisoned.

Many flowering plants are supported by the downland soils. Some, such as Orchids and Milkwort, are dependent on the calcium-rich soils and several species of insect such as the Common Blue and Chalkhill Blue butterflies feed exclusively off downland plants. There is also plenty of bird life to be seen, including Skylarks, Meadow Pipits, Lapwings and Corn Buntings which inhabit the areas of sparse cover. Yellowhammers populate the scrubland and the denser vegetation is the home of woodland birds.

Route Description:

1. From your parking place (GR.479840) follow The Ridgeway in an easterly direction, taking in the splendid views on either side of you and continue on under the A34 at Gore Hill.

2. *At Gore Hill, to the south is Sheep Down and to the north lie the villages of Upton and Chilton.* Follow The Ridgeway along a short concreted section of track and then turn right down the signposted byway. Ride along this track over East Ilsley Down to the main Compton/East Ilsley road.

3. Cross straight over this road and onto another byway which is known as Dennisford Road. Follow this byway for approximately 0.75 miles until you come to a crossroads in the tracks, at Shrill Down (GR.497799).

4. At the crossroads of tracks, turn left and follow Green Hams Lane which meanders through some pleasantly wooded scenery. After about 1.25 miles you will come to a junction of tracks (GR.503785).

5. Take the track signposted to your right and continue along this for about 0.33 miles until you come to an avenue of Beech trees.

6. At this junction, turn right and follow this path westwards. Eventually you will ride under the A34 and onto the Beedon road. Turn left here and follow this road up the short hill into Beedon.

7. Take the first right turn in Beedon and then turn immediately left down the bridleway. Ride along this bridleway for approximately 1.50 miles past the attractive cottages of Beedon Common and then at the gated byway, take the next right turn which takes you onto historic Old Street (GR.468767).

8. Follow Old Street Lane for about one mile, go across Hailey's Lane and then on past the tumulus at Barrow Hill. Where the track forks, take the left-hand track keeping Redland Wood to your right. Keep riding straight on along this track until you come to a small copse where the byway changes to a bridleway. Follow this bridleway across an open field to its junction with the road and turn right along the road. Three hundred yards along the road there is a sharp right-hand bend. Take the track directly in front of you. You are now back on Old Street. *Five hundred yards along Old Street there is a track leading off to the left. This is*

TRAIL 2.

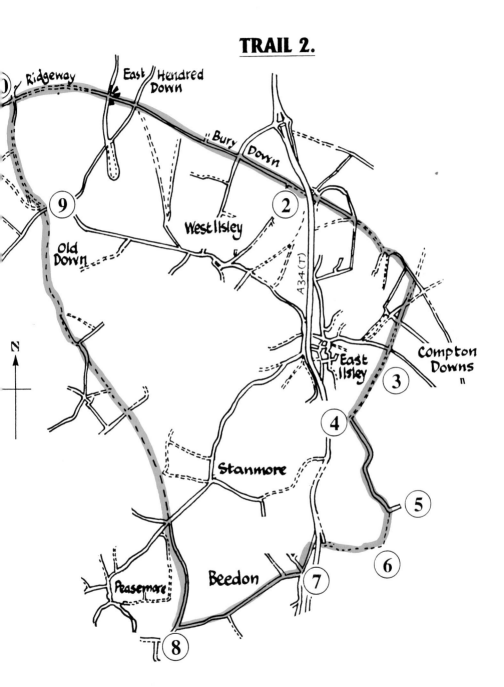

a RUPP known as Furze Lane. If you wish to make a detour into Farnborough then follow this track into the village. Keep riding along Old Street which now runs under a thick canopy of tree growth. *There is often heavy going here, but when the track opens out there are pleasant views over the Downs towards West Ilsley and Farnborough on either side.* Turn right here at West Ginge Down, and then immediately left up the waymarked bridleway at Lands End.

9.   Follow the bridleway to the summit where it joins The Ridgeway (GR.443850).

10.   At The Ridgeway, turn right and follow the trail back to the Bury Down car park, and your starting point.

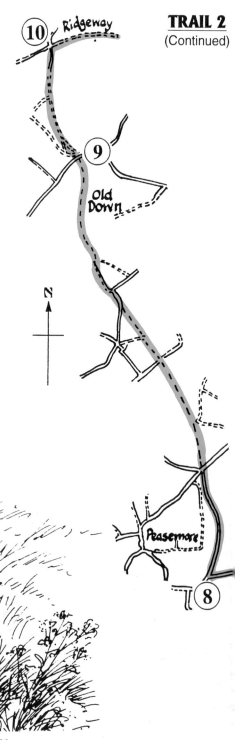

COMPTON/ASTON TIRROLD/ BLEWBURY

TRAIL 3

A 13 MILE CIRCULAR TRAIL (CLOCKWISE)

Ordnance Survey Maps:
Pathfinder:1155
Landranger: 174

Parking & Starting Point:
Parking is available near Superity Farm, Churn Road, Compton (GR. 515806), where there is a wide, firm grass byway for many horseboxes.

Parking Note: Parking and horse accommodation is also available at Blewbury Riding Centre by prior arrangement with Jane Dexter (0235) 851016. If you park here your trail will start from GR.536863.

Please do not ride on the gallops. There is plenty of space to canter on the bridleways and drove roads.

Route Description:

1.   Ride from Superity Farm and continue along the wide grassy byway with the concrete farm road on your right hand side and turn right at the signpost onto the Ridgeway track (GR.509819). *The lovely views of the Chiltern Hills are to the north-east and the Cotswolds are to the north-west.* Follow the track slightly downhill alongside the gallops, *(these gallops were used for the TV serial 'Trainer'),* crossing a bridge over the disused railway (GR.519824). Continue to follow the Ridgeway signs until you come to GR.526823 where you take the left fork off the Ridgeway track. *In the spring and summer, numerous 'down' flowers*

may be seen here. Continue straight ahead on this track to Lowbury Hill (GR.540823), *the site of a Roman temple,* and on to the Fair Mile, a wide drove road.

2.   Ride along this track until you come to the A417 Reading to Wantage road (GR.573838), where you CROSS WITH CARE to take the Cholsey road which is the left-hand fork. Continue along this track and at GR.575847 turn left to Lollingdon Farm (GR.570854) with its attractive red brick barns. Pass the farm on your right and continue west towards Aston Tirrold, *where you can see a Queen Anne house.* At the metalled road turn right, then in 100 yards, bear left to take the marked bridleway just before The Old Post Office (GR.556857). Follow this bridleway until you reach the road (GR.552862), where you turn right to ride along the road, following the garden wall of the farmhouse to the village. CARE, the road is narrow.

3.   Just before the Chequers Public House (GR.555862), turn left along Thorpe Lane and ride on until you come to the church (GR.554862). Go past the church, then immediately turn left off the metalled road; a white cottage is in front of you; and skirt the churchyard. Follow the lane until you come to the marked bridleway where you turn right *(do not go along the grass track which lies in front of you),* and pass under Blewburton Hill , *which is an ancient Iron Age village with Lynchet system.*

Ride through the busy farmyard at Winterbrook Farm to the B4016 Didcot road at Blewbury (GR.537860).

4.   Cross straight over the road *(if you have parked at Blewbury Riding Centre you turn right at this point)* and continue on to take the second turning right (GR.534860) and ride along this road through Blewbury village to come to the A417 Reading to Wantage road (GR.527856). *The Blewbury Inn is a few yards up the road and on your left.* Cross straight over the A417 WITH

CARE and go onto the marked bridlepath which takes you directly to Churn Farm (GR.510836). Turn right at the concrete farm road and then left at the metalled road.   Pass over the disused railway (GR.509832) and when you meet the fork in the track, go left up the grassy track which takes you up to the Ridgeway (GR.508821). On meeting the Ridgeway, turn left and ride alongside the concrete farm road and so return to your starting point at Superity Farm.

TRAIL 3.

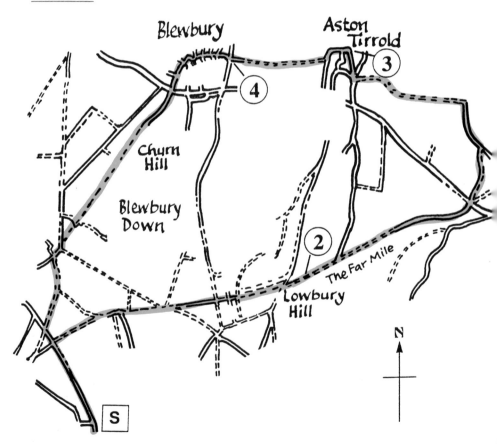

COMPTON/ALDWORTH/
HAMPSTEAD NORREYS/EAST ILSLEY

TRAIL
4

A 15 MILE CIRCULAR TRAIL (CLOCKWISE)

Ordnance Survey Maps:
Pathfinder: 1155 & 1171
Landranger: 174

Parking & Starting Point:
Parking is available at Superity Farm, Churn Road, Compton (GR.515806), where there is a wide, firm grass byway with parking for many horseboxes.

Route Description:

1.   From your parking point, ride in a north-westerly direction along the wide grassy byway keeping the concrete road on your right. Turn right onto the signposted Ridgeway track (GR.509819). Ride along the track and pass over the disused railway to continue along the Ridgeway for approximately three miles, following the numerous Ridgeway signposts. *There is beautiful rolling downland all around you, and good views to the Chiltern Hills on the left and to the Hampshire Downs on the right.* Turn right off the Ridgeway after passing a track on your left to Warren Farm (*the farm buildings can be seen on your left*), onto the stone byway (GR.550813) where there is a small triangle of grass. *The valley on the left is Streatley Warren.*

2.   Ride on down the byway until the track curves to the right; here you pass through the gate on the left into a (signposted) grassy field. Go through the gate on the far side of the field; the gate is situated just to the left of the line of telegraph poles. *This field*

sometimes has cattle in it. If you wish to avoid them, do not pass through the gate, but continue on the stone byway and ride into Aldworth to rejoin the route at GR.555793. Continue straight ahead and soon you come to a grassy track with a barbed wire fence on the right and an open field on the left, which then gives way to a stone track. Keep to the stone track and within 50/100 yards of reaching a tennis court on your left, at Westridge Green (GR.563798), turn right onto another stone track.

3.   Ride on down the track to meet the Aldworth to Streatley road (GR.563797), turn right onto the road and almost immediately turn left off the road onto a byway which lies between two hedges - there is a signpost but it can be difficult to see. Ride along this dirt track, *which, if the weather is wet, can be muddy in places,* for about one mile when you will meet a metalled road (GR.569788). *The countryside around you is now partially wooded.* Turn right onto the metalled road and then right again when you meet the Upper Basildon to Aldworth road (GR.566786). Continue on this road for about 0.50 miles then take the marked byway on the left (GR.561789). Ride along the byway until you meet the metalled road at Aldworth (GR.555792) then turn left onto the B4009 for 100 yards. When the road bends to the left, cross over, or go round, the grass triangle in front of you and take the narrow bridleway on the left-hand side of the white cottage which lies straight

23

in front of you (GR.555793). *(If you wish to visit Aldworth village, and the Bell Public House, take the road into the village, keeping the church on your left)*

4.   Ride along the narrow bridleway until you reach the Compton road (GR.548791) and cross onto a minor road which lies ahead of you and is signposted 'Hampstead Norreys & Hermitage'. Continue along this road for 1.50 miles to a T-junction (GR.528773) at the Compton-Hampstead Norreys road. *Here you have far reaching views to the south. CARE, visibility is good, but the road is*

sometimes busy. **Turn left then, after approximately 400 yards, turn right at a sign to Oak House Mill & Grain Store, opposite a house called Fiveways (GR.527768).** *If you wish to visit Hampstead Norreys, where there is a Public House, take the left fork at Fiveways and turn left at the mini-roundabout. After approximately 400 yards you will find the Public House on the left.*

5.   Follow the bridleway track up the hill which is straight in front of you. Pass Ramsworth Cottages on your left and ride on until you come to a filled-in cattle grid which you pass over. Here

TRAIL 4.

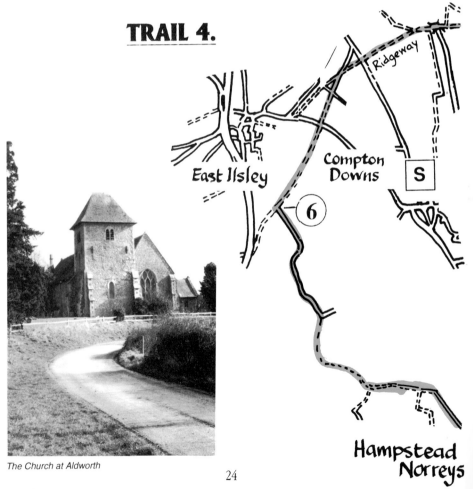

Ridgeway

East Ilsley

Compton Downs

S

6

The Church at Aldworth

Hampstead Norreys

24

the bridleway turns right, in front of Banterwick Farm (GR.509776) where you keep to the still well-defined track. Pass the old barn on your left and in approximately 100 yards the bridleway turns sharp left, along the farm side of the hedgerow where the track is not quite so well defined. On meeting a cross-roads of well-defined tracks (GR.503779), turn right into the grassy Green Hams Lane. Ride along the lane until the track forks, where you go to the left and along the woodland track to meet another cross-roads of tracks (GR.497799), and here you turn right onto a stone track. *If you wish to visit East Ilsley, where you will find three*

Public Houses, do not turn right here but go straight across to turn left when you reach the road and then right at the T-junction.

6.   Continue down the stone track until you meet the East Ilsley to Compton road (GR.504810) which you cross to continue on the track until you meet a very wide track on the left (GR.506816). Turn right onto this wide track   to   meet   the   Ridgeway (GR.509819) where you turn right and so keeping the concrete road to your left, return to your parking and starting point.

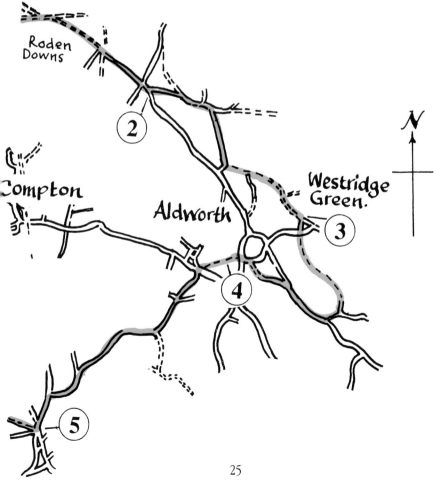

A 15 MILE CIRCULAR TRAIL (CLOCKWISE)

Ordnance Survey Maps:
Landranger: 174
Pathfinder: 1154 & 1170

Parking & Starting Point:
Parking is available at the Ridgeway Centre, Courthill (GR.394849). Your route is described from here.

Parking Note: The Ridgeway Centre at Courthill is close to the A338 Wantage to Hungerford road. It is a superior grade Youth Hostel with parking and stabling. The stabling is only suitable for smaller horses.

The Court Hill Youth Hostel and Ridgeway Centre

Route Description:

1.   From The Ridgeway Centre, ride to the A338.* Turn right onto the track between the hedge and fence and ride to a point on the road where there is a clear view for crossing to the left-hand side. Continue along the road for a short distance until you come to the signpost for The Ridgeway where you turn right along the track.

If you wish to avoid riding on A338, ride from the Youth Hostel to the A338 and cross over onto the track. Follow this track for one mile to join the signposted Ridgeway. Turn right onto the Ridgeway and ride on until you pass White House Farm and so reach the A338 again. Turn right along the road for a few yards then left onto the Ridgeway and continue as below.

2.   Pass Segsbury Farm on your left and at the next waymarked track, turn left (GR.381842). Cross a private drive to a farm, and then a dutch barn on the right and come to a more road-like surface. Continue along the track and where it bears left, continue straight on and onto a grass track past a trig point. Skirt left round the farm buildings and out onto the road to South Fawley.

3.   At the road turn right, signposted 'Eastbury and Warren Farm'. Ride downhill and at the bottom turn left along the signposted bridleway. Follow the chicken-wire fence of the poultry farm on the right and pass the tank on breeze blocks. Immediately after turn right still following the fence and ride into a woodland area.

4.   When almost to the tarmac road (GR.377789) take the signposted bridleway to the left. Where the hard surface bears left, ride straight on and along the left side of the field with the hedgerow on the left. At the field corner ride straight through the narrow gap in the hedge and bear left going onto a track between hedges.   When you reach the four-armed bridleway sign (GR.387783) turn right and ride across the field.   At the next signposted bridleway ride straight on across the field and onto a signposted bridleway between two hedges to reach a road (GR.369774).

5.   Turn right along the road and then turn onto the first track on the left just before the house. When reaching the gallops area at the top of the hill, ride straight on between the grass gallops on the left and the all-weather gallop on the right, behind the fence. *The track is wheelmarked and at the top end is funnelled between a broken hedge on the right and a blue-covered fence on the left.* At the T-junction, turn left and at the end of the hedge on the right, turn right with the electricity pole on the corner. At the top of the hill you will see a Larch tree just ahead (GR.367804), turn left here and then immediately right onto a track between barbed wire fences.

6.   Following the track, pass straight over a private road and continue until you come to a junction of cross tracks (GR.366829) where you turn right. Ride down this track until you reach a larger track where you bear left and ride to the signposted Ridgeway. On reaching the Ridgeway, turn right and follow this track until you get back to the A338. Turn left along the road and ride along the track behind the hedge until you come to the Youth Hostel and your parking place.

28

TRAIL 5.

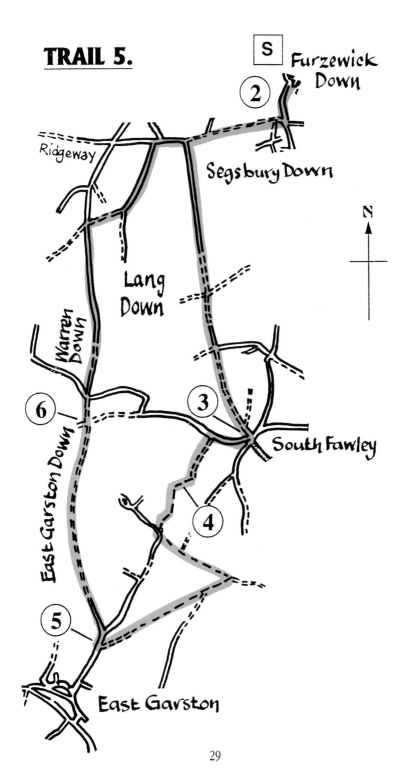

S Furzewick Down

Ridgeway

Segsbury Down

N

Lang Down

Warren Down

6

East Garston Down

3

South Fawley

4

5

East Garston

AROUND LAMBOURN

TRAIL 6

A 19 MILE CIRCULAR TRAIL (CLOCKWISE)

Ordnance Survey Maps:
Pathfinder: 1154 & 1170
Landranger: 174

Parking & Starting Point:
Parking is available on the Ridgeway, at the junction with the byway to the south-west and Sparsholt road to the north-east at GR.331858.

Route Description:

1.   Leave your parking place on the Ridgeway at GR.331858 and proceed riding east, then south-east along the Ridgeway, to turn right at the next junction onto a metalled road. Take the first left fork onto a grass byway which runs to the right and parallel to, a metalled farm road (GR.341846). *If you are cantering, take care not to startle any livestock which is often grazing in adjacent fields.* At the next junction, just past a large red barn on your right, veer slightly right heading south south-west, onto a byway which runs to the left of, and parallel to, a concrete farm road (GR.349817). The byway joins the concrete road near to the top of a hill, but also continues, *overgrown in places*, to emerge just over the brow of the hill at College Farmhouse (GR.344805).

2.   Here the track bends to the left to become a metalled road. Follow this, down the hill and take the next turn onto a signposted byway (GR.341801). You will pass a yellow gas H sign at the corner and just round the corner on your left, there is a small mail box on a

short concrete post. After approximately 100 yards, the metalled part of the track ends, but you continue on up the hill.

3.   Cross the metalled road at Starlight Farm (GR.343799) and continue up hill. At the top, turn right onto a byway *(the turn to your left and straight ahead provide access to private gallops)*. Ride along the track to pass superb stables on your right where the track joins a metalled road at Chipping Lodge, and continue on down hill to a T-junction (GR.335782). Turn left and go past a farm on your right, go round a bend, then turn right onto a signposted byway to immediately cross the River Lambourn (GR.336779). *The river is very narrow at this point.* Proceed up the hill to the top to bear right along the edge of a wood and follow on to the bottom corner of the field (GR.332767).

4.   Turn sharp left onto a signposted bridleway, again following the track along the edge of woodland. Just over the brow of the hill, turn sharp right onto a byway, following the line of the hedge which is first on your left and then on your right. Ignore the next right turn and carry straight on along the track which has trees on both sides.

5.   Remain on this track, ignoring any left or right turns until you come to the next T-junction where you turn right (GR.335756). Ride along the track until you come to the next crossroads where you turn left up a concrete road. *Just*

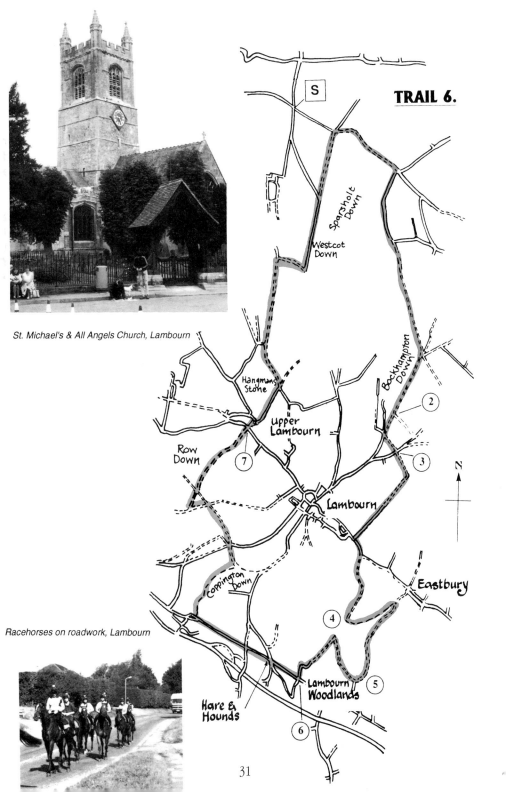

TRAIL 6.

S

Sparsholt Down

Westcot Down

Backhampton Down

2

3

N

St. Michael's & All Angels Church, Lambourn

Hangmans Stone

Upper Lambourn

Row Down

7

Lambourn

Coppington Down

Racehorses on roadwork, Lambourn

4

Eastbury

Lambourn Woodlands

5

Hare & Hounds

6

31

before you reach this junction, you will notice a thatched cottage to your right (GR.331763). When you reach Rooks Nest Estate, the track surface changes to metalled road, and as you continue on your way you will notice a mail box at the left on the wall of the house and the deer park on the right. Stay on the metalled road until you meet the B4000 Baydon to Newbury road where you turn right (GR.324756). A half-way lunch stop is possible here at the Hare & Hounds Public House on your left.

6. Your route continues along the B4000, to just past the large aerial mast on your left. Near the end of the straight section of road, turn right onto a metalled drive which is adjacent to a field gate through which you can see racing gallops with white railings. After about 100 yards, turn right onto a track which is just next to a green barn. When you reach the bottom of the hill, take a sharp left turn through a gate, which is normally left open, ignoring the gate on your right. Cross a metalled road (GR.310781) onto a byway and at the next crossroads, turn left, then right to ride through a pair of gates which you will usually find open. Carry straight on across the next byway junction and straight across the next metalled road junction (GR.313802).

7. Turn right at the next T-junction, then go left at the corner of a large building to turn left at the next byway junction (GR.320810). You will pass a track entering from the left; ignore this and carry on along the track to pass a barn on your left then go between the gallops you will find on both sides of you. At the end of the gallops take the next turning right and after passing the trees take the next turn left onto a straight section of metalled road. When

you come to the next left-hand bend, go straight ahead onto a byway (GR.328846) and on reaching the next T-junction turn right back onto The Ridgeway (GR.331858). You will find drinking water for yourself and a horse trough on the right just before you reach the end of the ride and your parking and starting point.

RIDGEWAY/CHADDLEWORTH/ PEASEMORE

TRAIL 7

A 25 MILE CIRCULAR TRAIL (CLOCKWISE)

Ordnance Survey Maps:
Landranger: 174
Pathfinder: 1155 & 1171

Parking & Starting Point:
Parking is available at the Wantage Monument (GR.425848) which is the start of your ride.

Parking Note: The parking at Wantage Monument is spacious and overlooks the amphitheatre of Lockinge Point-to-Point course. Parking, accommodation and stabling can be found at The Ridgeway Centre (GR.395851).

Of Interest:
Approximately two miles into the ride a small copse on the right offers superb views. If you look through the trees, you will see a long barrow, Scutchamer Knob; like Wayland's Smithy to the west, this is truly 'a tomb with a view', and contrasting views at that. To the north one can see the industrial complex of Didcot Power Station with its steaming cooling towers and immediately below is the significant collection of buildings that make up Harwell Atomic Research Establishment. However, to the south the landscape is apparently untouched since Celt and Saxon laid their dead to rest.

This ride can be done in reverse in which case The Harrow at West Ilsley makes an excellent refreshment point, and then gives an opportunity for a gallop up hill to The Ridgeway. With few exceptions the route is well signed.

Route Description:

1.   From your parking place ride east along the Ridgeway for approximately two miles, crossing Betterton Down, until the track narrows and becomes muddy where it passes a small copse on the right. *This is the point to see the views described above.* Continue your ride for a further half mile, riding beyond Scutchamer Knob. Here the huge sweeps of grass gallops disappear off down the hillside and you can see a neat signposted bridlepath on the right, which runs gently downhill (GR.463848).

2.	Turn along this trail and follow it all the way to West Ilsley. *This is a very picturesque village with its half-timbered buildings, 'The Harrow' Public House and adjacent duck pond.* Pass The Harrow, and ride eastwards down the village street for a few hundred yards until you see a byway sign on the right (GR.477823). Turn right along the byway which leads through a training yard and follow a metalled road with stud rail fencing on each side. After passing the buildings, turn right along the signposted bridlepath. Shortly afterwards at another set of signposts, the track becomes a pleasant grass path which you follow, turning left and then right into a copse.

3.	The ride comes out into a field with a barn on the right - *this is marked as Woolvers Barn on the map.* Follow the bridleway across the field and go between two wooden gate posts and into an old quarry. Ride past Redlane Barn and into Old Street, which becomes narrow and muddy before it emerges onto the Stanmore to Peasemore road, where you turn right (GR.468783).

4.	*The downland landscape has now been exchanged for a wood enclosed countryside although at every turn the sweep of the downs can be seen as a contrasting backdrop.* Follow the quiet road down into Peasemore. *Here you will notice the fine spire of the church which stands in silhouette on the left.* Take the first turn left in Peasemore and then turn right at the sign to Leckhampstead and Chaddleworth; after a few hundred yards you will pass The Fox and Hounds - *a fine-looking Public House. The 'pub' sign is interesting, it depicts a relaxed fox watching a pack of hounds that are obviously posing him little threat. There is a useful patch of grass opposite and real ales and fine wines are advertised.*

5.	To continue your ride, go down the hill where the road emerges into an open green with a 'cart track' sign on the right; turn here and ride up, and then down, this byway until it meets the Wantage to Newbury road at 'Egypt' and ride on into Leckhampstead. *On the green here there is an unusually grand War Memorial with a clock; also another public house 'The Stag', which would be good for a mid-day snack.* There are some pretty cottages in The Thicket on the Chaddleworth road, which you follow for a mile or so before the road crosses the Brightwalton junction and into Chaddleworth. Turn left along the main road and then right onto the bridleway known as Wick Lane. *(Alternatively, continue down the metalled lane into the village. Whichever way you choose, if the time of day is appropriate, call at The Ibex, a renowned hostelry kept by Colin Browne, Desert Orchid's first jockey.)*

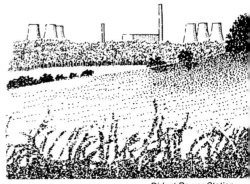

Didcot Power Station

34

TRAIL 7.

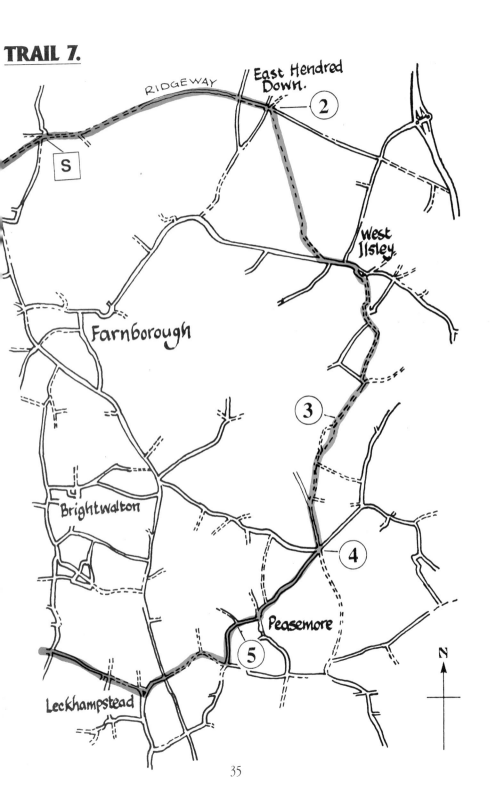

6.   Having passed The Ibex, take the Farnborough road through the village passing the fine Manor House and the old church which can be seen across a tennis court and an old walled kitchen garden. Just after the village boundary the road drops downhill and on the right hand bend you will see a bridleway off to the left. Turn left onto the bridleway. *The surface has been adapted with motorway shavings for racehorses to use, so looks a bit strange.* Take advantage of this track which follows the roadside hedge to the left and go straight across first the lane and then the main road to Henley Farm (GR.394782).

7.   From Henley Farm, take the unmarked byway up the hill and past a very pretty farmhouse. Then follow the waymarked bridleway along a narrow hedge boundary to come to a four-way signpost. Carry straight on along the narrow hedge track until it bends round into a field headland and emerges onto a stony track. Ride straight on to another junction and take a small muddy path into a copse, which will take you downhill for approximately 0.50 miles to come out alongside a huge, free-range poultry farm. Continue to follow the boundary fence round to the left to meet the metalled road (GR.385802).

8.   At the road, turn right and ride up the hill to the left and into South Fawley to the small green surrounded by farm cottages. *On the right here you can see the ancient Manor House just a short distance away.* Ride over to the black barn and take the track that goes between this and the farm machinery on the right and continue until the track becomes grass - *this is a good place for a canter.* At the next junction you will see a burnt-out barn which looks just like a piece of modern, abstract sculpture; pass this to the left and carry on for another two miles passing Letcombe Bowers farm to emerge on to the Ridgeway opposite the huge Hill Fort of Segsbury, or Letcombe Castle (GR.381841)- *like the one at Uffington. This is where the Bronze Age tribesmen gathered their families and flocks in times of danger.*

9.   From here, follow the Ridgeway eastwards for approximately three miles, crossing two main roads with care. *Once more you can enjoy the panorama of the Vale of the White Horse and the rolling Downlands to the south which are bisected by gallops but unsullied by any unsightly works of man. They refresh the soul and uplift the heart.* To return back to your parking and starting point.

36

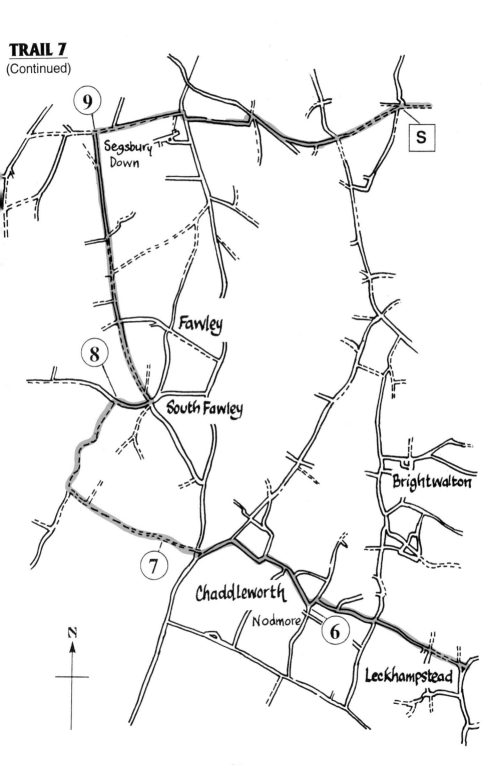

GREAT SHEFFORD/ EASTBURY

TRAIL 8

A 10 MILE CIRCULAR RIDE (CLOCKWISE)

Ordnance Survey Maps:
Landranger: 174
Pathfinder: 1170

Parking & Starting Point:
Parking is available alongside the bridleway (GR.379753) which is situated on the road between Eastbury and Great Shefford, approximately one mile outside Eastbury. The bridleway is signposted on the right-hand side.

Route Description:

1. Leave your starting point (GR.379753) and follow the track past houses and through a gateway and turn right. Follow the track round to the left keeping to the line of the hedge to the right. At the wire fence, carry straight on but with the hedge now on your left. Continue on the track which becomes gravel and passes several houses.

2. When you meet the T-junction at the bottom of the hill, turn right (GR.358738) and, after passing a barn, keep straight on following the track until it meets the B4000 at Fishers Farm (GR.358737). Turn right along this road - *CARE, the traffic can be fast* - and in approximately 0.50 miles at the second set of crossroads, turn right (GR.341747). *This is signposted Unsuitable for Motor Vehicles.* Keep on this lane until you see a signposted bridleway to the left (GR.346761). Turn along this bridleway and follow it until

you come to the third track on the right. Take this right turning and follow the track into a wood and across a small field. At the edge of the field turn right and keep going along the unmarked byway into Eastbury. In Eastbury, turn right. *Here you will find The Plough Public House which offers a good refreshment stop.*

3. On meeting the crossroads and the thatched barn, turn left signposted Eastbury Grange and follow the lane for 1.75 miles. At the signpost for Private Road, take the track on the right and at the next byway sign turn right keeping to the right-hand track going up the hill. When you come to the next T-junction, turn right and pass Cranes Farm (GR.359779). Keep to the right-hand track past Pounds Farmhouse and so on to meet the road.

4. Follow this road past a sharp right-hand bend and then take the next left turn, signposted 'Byway' (GR.378788). Keep to the right-hand track and follow this until you reach Maidencourt Farm. Ride up the farm drive and onto the road. At the road, turn left (GR.372757) - *CARE as traffic can be fast* - and follow the road back to your starting point.

38

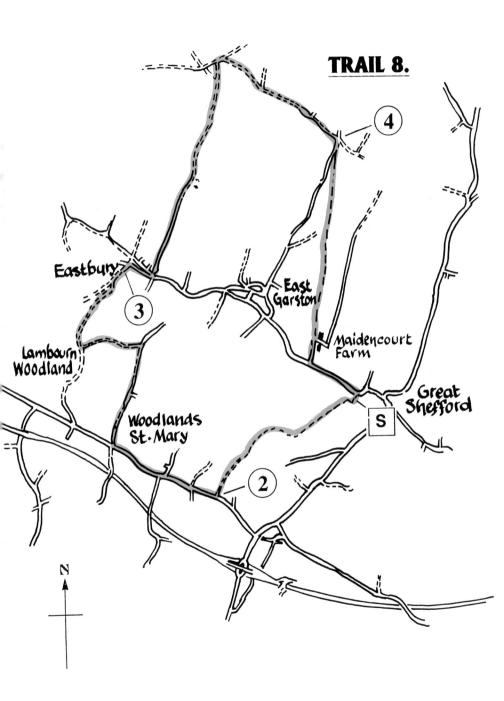

TRAIL 8.

④

Eastbury

③

East
Garston

Maidencourt
Farm

Lambourn
Woodland

Great
Shefford

Woodlands
St. Mary

S

②

N

39

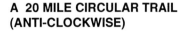

TRAIL 9

A 20 MILE CIRCULAR TRAIL (ANTI-CLOCKWISE)

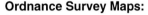

Ordnance Survey Maps:
Landranger: 174
Pathfinder: 1170

Parking and Starting Point:
Parking is available around the square in Aldbourne but this can get busy. Your starting point is also here at GR.264757

Route Description:

1.   From your starting point in the square at Aldbourne (GR.264757), head south and follow the road, by the side of the garage, signposted for Axbridge. Turn left into The Butts and keep going through Southward Lane. When you come to the byway signs, take the far left track which is signposted Ramsbury. Ride on down this track until you reach the end (GR.275716) and turn left. On reaching the crossroads, pass The Bell Public House (GR.276716) and cross straight over.

2.   Turn right at the signpost to Froxfield (GR.278716), and when you see the signpost for Littlecote House turn left, keeping to the left on this track, following the blue arrows. *At Littlecote there is a coffee shop and toilets on the left hand side of the village.* Keep going through Littlecote following the 'Way Out' signs to turn left along the road out at GR.321700.

3.   On reaching the T-junction (GR.323703), in Chilton Foliat, turn right towards Leverton and take the next turn left (GR.333700) to Old Hayward-

passing by a row of thatched cottages. Take the right turn (GR.336709) to New Hayward Farm - *there are water troughs along this track.* After you pass the farm buildings, turn left, then left again onto the metalled road (GR.342709) and ride in a north-easterly direction. When you reach the T-junction (GR.345715) turn left, then right towards Poughley.

4.   At the top of the hill turn left where you see an old signpost for 'Cart Track' at GR.345726, and keep straight on, heading for a small opening in the wood. Take the single track straight on, to come onto a track on the right hand side of the field. *This track is not always well used, so it can get overgrown. Look out for deer along here.* Keep straight on until you reach the main road, taking care as you cross over the motorway bridge. At the main road turn right and then left at GR.342745.

5.   After the wood, take the second turning left. Continue on to take the third track left into the wood and on across a small field. When you come to the T-junction, take the track to the left, and at the next junction turn right (GR.335755). Carry straight on at the crossroads into a lane. *This is Lambourn so there are lots of stables!*

6.   At the next junction turn left (GR.326787) and then take the next right, turning left at the crossroads and taking the next left again for Baydon (GR.325789). Continue on until you come to Farncombe Farm on the right-

hand side of the road and take the byway to the right (GR.311781). At the crossroads on the track turn left (GR.306788) - *there is no signpost.* Keep straight on past the farm to join the road and at the end of the road turn left over the motorway bridge (GR.281787).

7. When you meet the crossroads, go straight over into Aldbourne Road and keep going until you see the bridleway sign on the left for Preston (GR.278774). Keep straight on, even where the track goes off to the left. At the next T-junction (GR.277753), turn right down the hill and when you reach the main road, turn right and back to your starting point.

TRAIL 9.

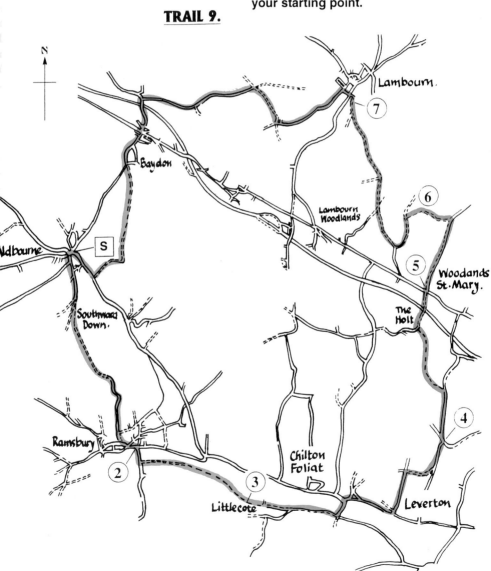

41

ALDBOURNE/ LIDDINGTON HILL RIDE

TRAIL 10

A 20 MILE CIRCULAR TRAIL (ANTI-CLOCKWISE)

Ordnance Survey Maps:
Landranger: 174
Pathfinder: 1154 & 1170

Parking and Starting Point:
Parking is available in the lay-by next to the Shepherds Rest Public House, which is on the Ridgeway at GR.231813. This is also your starting point.

Route Description:

1.   Leave your parking area at GR.231813 riding in a south-westerly direction and follow the road sign for Liddington, which takes you over the motorway bridge. At the road junction (GR.218807), turn left on B4192 and go up the hill where you turn right at the top onto the bridleway (GR.218804) to follow the stony path. Go through the gate, keeping to the track, and continue on riding through three more gates. *Enjoy the lovely views up here.* After going through the third gate, keep to the left of the fields and ride straight on past the bridleway sign and 'The Ridgeway' sign. As you reach the junction on the track (GR.214774), turn left - *there is no sign here* - and join a concrete road that will take you past some farm buildings.

CHARLBURY FARM STABLES

Escorted rides, for all ages and abilities, on our own horses.
Easy access to all Ridgeway Rides.
Picnic rides a speciality.
Lessons from BHSAI by arrangement.
We can also book farmhouse bed & breakfast nearby if required.

Mrs. Charlotte Swann
Charlbury Farm Stables
Hinton Parva, Nr. Swindon
Wilts. SN4 0DL

Telephone: 0793 790065
0793 790532

42

2.   Ride on past houses and turn right, going through a metal gate which has a 'No Parking' sign on it. Continue on until you reach the next gate to ride through the field bearing slightly right to the gate and following the track on through fields until you meet the B4192 (GR.255763). Turn right here and go along the road into Aldbourne. *There is a shop and public house in the village.*

3.   Take the left turn for Baydon/ Lambourn and then go left again up a narrow lane towards the Church. Continue straight on going past the backs of houses and crossing straight over two metalled roads to meet a stony track. Ride along this track to the end (GR.263790).

4.   When you come to a metalled road, cross straight over and into the field where the bridleway runs diagonally across towards the motorway bridge. Follow the bridleway and cross over the bridge and then go left into a field to follow the track on the right hand side of the field. *DO NOT GO ON TO THE PRIVATE GALLOPS!*

5.   Keep to the track on the right, passing through a gate, to eventually reach The Ridgeway (GR.235816). Turn left and after a short distance rejoin the road to take you back to your starting point.

TRAIL 10.

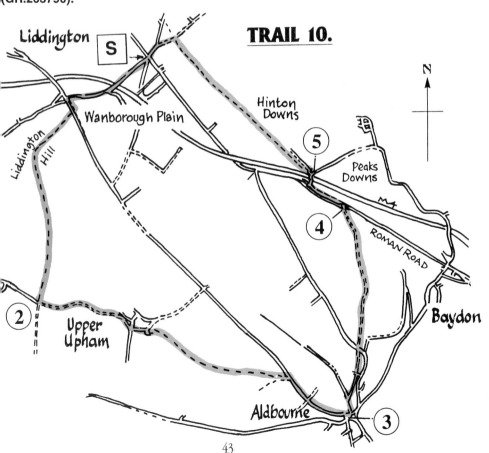

RUSSLEY PARK

TRAIL 11

A 15 MILE CIRCULAR TRAIL (CLOCKWISE)

Ordnance Survey Maps:
Pathfinder: 1154 & 1170
Landranger: 174

Parking & Starting Point:
Parking is available in the lay-by next to the Shepherds Rest Public House, which is on the Ridgeway at GR231813. This is also your starting point.

Of Interest:
Please note that there are no other public houses on this route. If you wish you may make a one mile detour from Upper Lambourn for refreshments in Lambourn. This is the half-way point on your ride. You may also wish to note that the ride includes several closed gates. However, most of these can be opened and closed whilst mounted. Please be sure to close any field gates that you have opened.

Route Description:

1.   **Ride from the Shepherds Rest Public House at GR.231813 and turn left up the hill to take the first right turn along the Ridgeway. The route continues straight along the Ridgeway for about four miles ignoring all left and right turns until you come to Wayland's Smithy (GR.285855).** *The first crossing you meet is the metalled Bishopstone road (GR.252827) and the second is the Idstone track (GR.264835). Drinking water and a horse trough are provided at the Idstone track a few yards along the left turn. Your next crossing is the metalled* **Ashbury to Lambourn road (GR.274843) and then the unmarked Odstone track crossing. Wayland's**

Smithy then appears on your left (GR.285855). It is fenced and gated and shadowed by large Beech trees.

2.   Take the next track right and continue along this route going all the way to Upper Lambourn which is just under four miles. Ignore all left and right turnings. *The track surface changes from rough stone to good grass. However, adjacent verges and in places, parallel grass tracks, provide good alternatives to bad stony sections. Enjoy some good canters along the grass strips.*

3.   The track becomes a metalled road at the outskirts of Upper Lambourn (GR.303820) and there are useful verges here and there. Pass several racing stables on both sides and follow the road round a sharp bend to the right followed by a sharp bend left. Take the next right turn to go up hill towards the B4000 (GR.316804). Ride across this road onto a metalled road which is signed 'Row Down Nos. 7-12', keeping the farm buildings on your left. After about 300 yards, continue to ride up hill along the track. *There are private gallops at the top, so watch out for racehorses.* Take the next turn right (GR.304791), where it is neatly hedged on both sides. When the hedge ends, do not be tempted to follow the track to the left, but continue straight forward onto an unmarked grass bridleway which takes you across the private gallops - *again beware of racehorses.* Continue along this grass track still going up hill and then head for the gated area straight ahead (GR.298799). Ride

through the gateway and down the steep hill to turn right at the bottom. Follow the track to the next crossroads (GR.291803) and turn left through a gate, onto a bridleway. Stay on this track, ignoring all left and right turns to go through another gate which is close to a wood on your right. Ride straight on to go through the next gate and across grass to another gate and then follow the line of the fence on your left.

4.   Pass through the next gate, which is near a water trough, and then go through yet another gate close to some farm buildings (GR.270799) to meet a metalled road. Ignore the turning to your left and continue straight on along the metalled road seeing Russley Park on your right. When you come to the top of the hill and the M4 motorway bridge (GR.259795), turn right and go through the small wooden gate which is next to a larger metal gate to turn immediately right. *Do not follow the line of the motorway fence and keep away from the gallops.*

5.   Then turn left onto a bridleway and ride straight on ignoring all junctions. Continue up Fox Hill (GR.235813) and ride between the gate posts (the gate is missing!), keeping to the right of the aerial mast, and back onto The Ridgeway (GR.236816). Turn left here and left again to return to the Shepherds Rest Public House and your starting point.

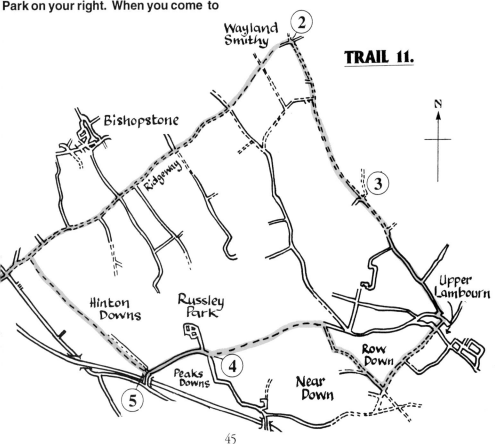

45

DOWN BARN FARM

A hundred acre grass farm in the depths of the Downs.
One single and one double bedroom. Bed, breakfast, grass and
stable livery. Dinner and escorted rides by arrangement.
Miles of off-road riding and plenty of good pubs nearby.

Down Barn Farm,
Sparsholt Down, Sparsholt,
Wantage OX12 9XD
Tel: 0367 820272

The Country Code should be observed by every rider, with great care being taken to keep to the line of the Public Rights of Way particularly when crossing farmland.

A 11 MILE CIRCULAR RIDE (ANTI-CLOCKWISE)

Ordnance Survey Maps:
Landranger: 174
Pathfinder: 1154 & 1170

Parking & Starting Point:
Parking is available at the car park at Sparsholt Firs (GR.343851) on the Lambourn to Wantage/Sparsholt Road, which is your starting point. Parking is also available at White Horse Hill (GR.296865).

Parking Note: Sparsholt Firs is a misleading name since there are many more Beeches than Firs. The best landmark being the huge disc of the radio mast which lies 100 yards south of the car park (GR.343851). If parking at the car park on White Horse Hill (GR.296865) your ride will start at paragraph three of the description and, having followed to the end of the description, return to your parking via paragraphs one and two of the route!

Route Description:

1.	From your parking place at Sparsholt Firs (GR.343851) ride immediately west along the Great Ridgeway, with Lambourn gallops and fields on the left and the Vale of the White Horse spread out like a map on the right.

2.	After 0.75 miles, having gone down a dip and straight across a byway crossing, The Ridgeway crosses the Lambourn/Kingston Lisle road at the top of Blowing Stone Hill and gradually ascends towards the White Horse Hill.

If you have parked in the car park at White Horse Hill (GR.296865), ride up the small metalled road, keeping to the right on the turf as the Ridgeway is slippery, bare chalk at this point.

3.	The ride continues with all riders now turning left (GR.300861) to follow the well signposted bridleway at the top of the rise on The Ridgeway track. This will take you alongside fields and through two small gateways and so on to a bridleway that runs to the right of a splendid gallop. *This belongs to the famous old training establishment of Kingstone Warren.* After approximately 0.75 miles, the bridleway narrows and turns left through a gap. Go through the gap and turn immediately right (GR.308839) to ride down Whit Coombe Hill, bearing right and then left and left again at the byways crossroads (GR.299827) at Park Farm. *Park Farm is distinguished by the rather muddy track in front of it and there is usually a lot of machinery lying around outside.*

4.	Follow the track which becomes a small, slippery, metalled road as you pass Maddle Farm on the left. *It is suggested that you ride on the grass verge as the surface has been worn to a glass-like sheen by the feet of the hundreds of race-horses going to and from the gallops. Indeed, you are likely to meet some strings coming to and*

47

TRAIL 12.

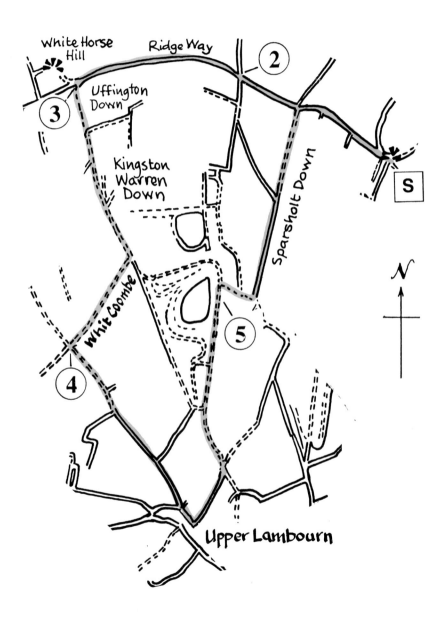

White Horse Hill

Ridge Way

②

③

Uffington Down

Kingston Warren Down

Sparsholt Down

White Coombe

④

⑤

S

N

Upper Lambourn

from the yards in Upper Lambourn. Having followed this track for about one mile, take the second turn left onto a metalled road with a good grass verge and ride up the hill alongside all-weather and grass gallops, to Hangmans Stone. Here the byways divide. Follow the right hand track which becomes bordered by trees. Pass a dutch barn and continue to emerge alongside another gallop above Seven Barrows, *which is both the name of the archaeological site and Nicky Henderson's training yard, the oldest in Lambourn, founded in 1878.*

5.   Follow the all-weather track down the hill and turn right to meet a road. *From here you can see The Seven Barrows, both mound and 'cup and saucer', which are more than 2000 years old. This is a natural history site and although fenced off, it is possible to go through the fence and examine them at close quarters.* Follow the road round to the right and turn left onto the uphill track. At the end of the track you will meet the road just below Sparsholt Radio Mast, alongside Eastmanton Down gallop, and your starting point at Sparsholt Firs lies just north of here.

If you started from White Horse Hill, you must follow the first two paragraphs in order to return to your parking place.

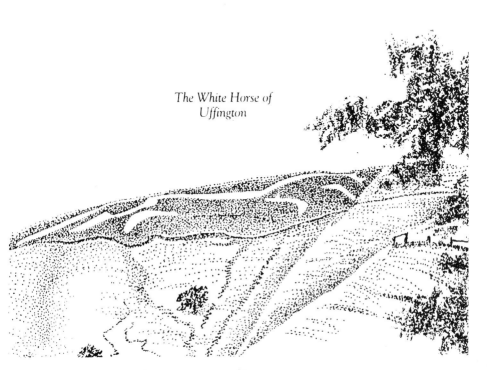

The White Horse of
Uffington

49

LOCKINGE DOWN/ FARNBOROUGH/CATMORE/ LILLEY/BRIGHTWALTON

TRAIL 13

A 10 MILE CIRCULAR ROUTE (ANTI-CLOCKWISE)

Ordnance Survey Maps:
Landranger: 174
Pathfinder: 1155

Parking & Starting Point:
Parking is available at Lockinge Kiln Farm, Lockinge on the B4494 at Wantage, just south of the Ridgeway (GR.423833) and your ride starts from here.

Parking Note: Lockinge Kiln Farm, Lockinge is owned by Mr & Mrs Cowan. However, although the farm offers Bed & Breakfast, it is also a busy, working pig and sheep farm. Parking is limited but secure.

Of Interest:
Farnborough is the highest village in Berkshire. The Poet Laureate, John Betjeman, used to live in the truly gem-like Queen Anne Manor. It is a charming building and now inhabited by the well-known Peer and journalist - Lord Oaksey. The church is worth a visit as it has a beautiful stained glass window, designed by John Piper, in memory of his friend; the poet.

Route Description:

1. From Lockinge Kiln Farm (GR.423833) ride down the farm drive and bear to the right round a rubble heap and a Beech tree to join the unmarked track as it goes south-east to Farnborough. *This byway is just over the Oxfordshire county boundary.* The definitive line of the track actually lies across Mr Cowan's sheep paddock,

just to the right of the entrance to the farm. You enter the field by a metal gate and exit on the other side by another metal gate. However, the farmer encourages riders to follow the route described to join the track.

2. *The pleasant track is rather overgrown, but in season it is thick with blackberries and elderberries. On your left you will pass the inappropriate but picturesquely named 'Moonlight Barn' with its rusty metal roof.* At the end of the track turn left (GR.430820) and follow the road into Farnborough and ride straight through the village, perhaps pausing to look at the church.

3. Follow the road round a corner where you will see a large farm. Look for, and follow, the waymarked byway which you will notice is little used. The ride enters a copse which you ride straight through and look for a four-way bridlepath signpost to take the Parkwood track. You are now at Old Street, an ancient drove road which at this point, can be muddy. Go across into Parkwood and join the Catmore road a little further up and turn right (GR.456814). *The way through Parkwood is very pleasant and avoids the 'swamps' of Old Street.* Ride through the tiny village of Catmore - *there is a large farm, a small house and a venerable church* - and from there ride on into Lilley. *Note the private dwelling with its Toby Jug figure - this indicates where the Public House used to be.*

TRAIL 13.

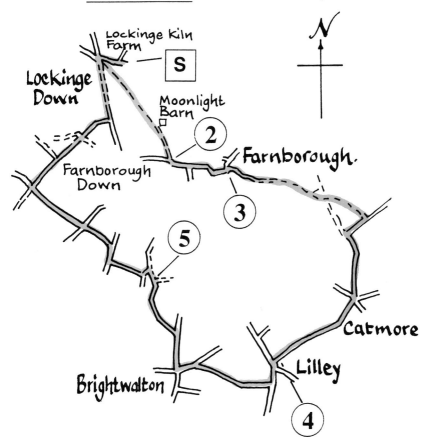

4. Take the second turning on the left (GR.443796) and then go right into Long Lane and follow it towards Brightwalton where you will see two corrugated-iron sheds. The byway is marked to the right of these. This is Browns Lane. Follow the lane to the next junction where you bear left and continue along to come to Brightwalton Common (GR.428806).

5. Turn left onto a metalled road and then, almost immediately, go right down a signposted byway, passing beneath a grove of Sycamore trees and onto a small, metalled lane. At the next

junction turn left (GR.422810). *This is signposted 'Farnborough Down Farm Only', but it is not a private road.* Take the tree-lined estate road, keeping off the grass verges please, and ride into this secret valley where you can see the lovely neo-classical house built by the estate owner. Keep straight on up the hill past the houses until the unclassified road you are on is bisected by an unmarked byway. Turn right (GR.411818) and when you come to the next crossroads, ride straight on to return to Lockinge Kiln Farm and your parking place.

SAFETY

**Know your Highway Code
(1994 Edition)**

**In Particular
Paragraphs 216/224**

FOLLOWING A ROUTE

The descriptions given in this book were correct at the time of printing but it should be borne in mind that landmarks and conditions can change. It is assumed every user will carry and be competent in the use of the appropriate Ordnance Survey Pathfinder or Landranger map. This is essential as the route may not be waymarked along the whole of its length.

52

WANTAGE MONUMENT

A 9 MILE CIRCULAR RIDE (ANTI-CLOCKWISE)

Ordnance Survey Maps:
Landranger: 174
Pathfinder: 1155

Parking & Starting Point:
Parking & Starting Point:
Parking is available on the grass verge where the B4494 crosses The Ridgeway, south of Wantage (GR.418841) at the view point adjacent to the entrance to Wantage Monument, your starting point.

Of Interest:
The Wantage Monument, raised to a Victorian Baron Wantage, provides a proper landmark, although the radio mast on the road to the south is even more salient in this sweeping landscape. The route lies through the well marked bridlegate into a large grass field which is, for a few occasions in the year, an amphitheatre car park for the drama staged on the Lockinge Point to Point course which is at the bottom of the hill. The ride will show you a wealth of historical and interesting features.

Route Description:

1.   Leaving the Wantage Monument, follow the waymarked bridleway into a large grass field and ride to the bottom of the hill where you will find a bridlegate. Go through the bridlegate and onto the Lockinge Point-to-Point course to follow the route heading south, alongside the shrouded jumps. Gradually the track becomes gravel and you will encounter two cattle grid crossings as you continue along the route. After about one mile you will see

to the right, the terraced mound of Arn Hill, a Saxon Burial mound, and your trail reaches an elegant equestrian establishment, with racehorse heads peering out of the fine old barns. *Those with any interest in National Hunt Racing will recognize the initials HK which are on the sheets worn by many of the exercising racehorses you may encounter.*

Any doubts about reasons to leave the open spaces of the Ridgeway heights to descend into the lower villages should soon be dispelled by the elegant parks, gardens and picturesque village buildings that have grown up over the centuries in this sheltered valley.

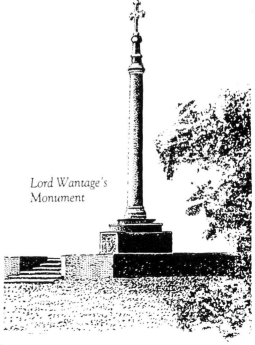

Lord Wantage's Monument

53

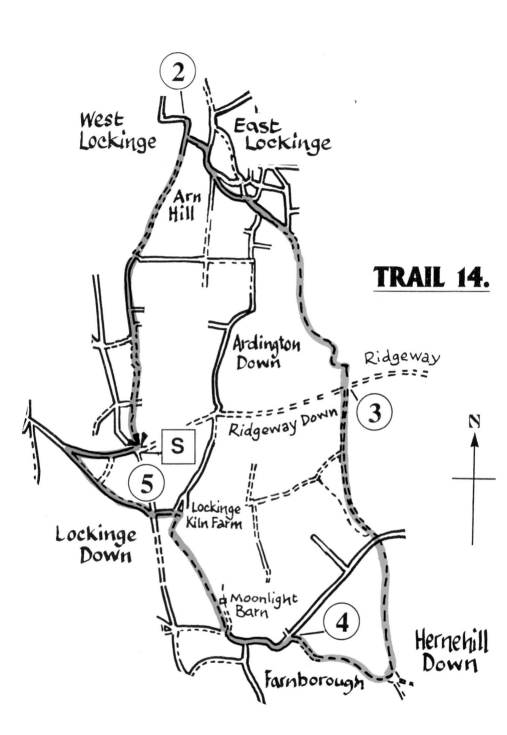

West Lockinge

East Lockinge

Arn Hill

TRAIL 14.

Ardington Down

Ridgeway

Ridgeway Down

S

Lockinge Down

Lockinge Kiln Farm

N

Moonlight Barn

Farnborough

Hernehill Down

54

2. Leave the training stables and still following the waymarked route, *spare a moment to look to the right to enjoy the fine park trees which are particularly attractive in autumn with the Beeches and others changing colour.* Keep following the village road to the right, past Lockinge Stud and more elegant equines, and then ride over a wooden bridge across the Lockinge Brook. *The brook winds all through the valley being fashioned into lakes and ornamental watergardens as it passes through parks and gardens.* At the next junction, take the right-hand fork to Betterton (GR.425873). Go through the farm where you will see the waymark sign pointing your route up the hill to the Ridgeway and West Ginge Down beyond. At the top of the hill, there is a series of copses to ride through - *you may glimpse the beautiful spotted rump of a Fallow deer amongst the golden Beech leaves.*

3. At The Ridgeway (GR.443850), there is a good crossroads sign. Follow the gravel track down the hill past the Down Barn Keeper's Cottage and so come to the white house at Lands End. Cross the road, and ride up the grassy track which wiggles amongst hedgerows and is sometimes muddy. Continue along here for about 100 yards and then go up onto the bank on the right. Keep bearing right into a neck of woodland until you meet an obvious track which is the byway to Farnborough. This is fairly overgrown, but a pleasant ride and you will come to the machine-strewn Upper Farm. Turn left onto the road (GR.438820). *Farnborough is the highest village in Berkshire and is notable for its church with a fine, modern, stained glass window designed by John Piper in memory of John Betjeman who lived at*

the Manor House. You can see the Queen Anne Manor House on your right, just before reaching the church.

4. Follow the village streets, pass the next three-way junction and ride straight on until you see a byway sign on the right (GR.430820) where you turn right. This track leads past the picturesquely-named, but rustily-roofed 'Moonlight Barn' and then goes down a slope until it reaches Lockinge Kiln Farm. Here the right of way leads through a metal gate, across a paddock and out onto the Wantage road via another gate. However, this paddock is often full of sheep and the very friendly farmer is happy for riders to go into the farmyard and bear left round a Beech tree with rubble at its foot and up the concrete drive to meet the road (GR.420834).

5. Almost straight across the road is an opening which, although unsigned, marks the entrance of a byway. Take this track and follow it for about 0.50 miles straight up to the Ridgeway to come out west of the Wantage Monument car park. The road back to the Monument is just a few hundred yards to the right and this will take you back to your parking place.

It is possible to go straight up the road from Lockinge Kiln Farm, but this route is quite narrow and busy and only recommended to those with traffic-proof mounts who are in a hurry!!

CODE FOR RIDING & DRIVING RESPONSIBLY

THE BRITISH
HORSE SOCIETY

1. **Riders and carriage drivers** everywhere should proceed with courtesy, care and consideration. The British Horse Society recommends the following:

    Care for the Land
    Do not stray off the line of the path;
    Do not damage timber or hedgerows by jumping;
    Remember that horses' hooves can damage surfaces in bad weather;
    Pay particular attention to protected areas that have significant historical and/or biological value, as they are extremely sensitive to damage.

    Courtesy to other users
    Remember that walkers, cyclists and other riders may be elderly, disabled, children or simply frightened of horses; whenever possible acknowledge courtesy shown by drivers of motor vehicles.

    Consideration for the farmer
    Shut the gate behind you;
    Ride slowly past all stock;
    Do not ride on cultivated land unless the right of way crosses it;
    Dogs are seldom welcome on farmland or moorland unless on a lead or under close control.

2. **Observe local byelaws**

3. **Ride or drive with care on the roads** and take the BHS Riding and Road Safety Test. Always make sure that you can be seen at night or in bad visibility, by wearing the right kind of reflective/ fluorescent aids.

4. **Groups from riding establishments** should contain reasonable numbers, for reasons of both safety and amenity. They should never exceed twenty in total **including** the relevant number of escorts as indicated in BHS guidelines on levels of capability among riders in groups, available on request. Rides should not deviate from the right of way or permitted route and regard must be shown at all times for growing crops, shutting and securing of gates and the consideration and courtesy due to others.

5. **Always obey the Country Code in every way possible:**
    Enjoy the countryside and respect its life and work
    Guard against all risk of fire
    Fasten all gates
    Keep your dogs under close control
    Keep to public paths across farmland
    Use gates and stiles to cross fences, hedges and walls
    Leave livestock, crops and machinery alone
    Take your litter home
    Help keep all water clean
    Protect wildlife, plants and trees
    Take special care on country roads
    Make no unnecessary noise.

RIDGEWAY CENTRE/
FARNBOROUGH/WEST ILSLEY

A 16 MILE CIRCULAR TRAIL
(ANTI-CLOCKWISE)

Ordnance Survey Maps:
Landranger: 174
Pathfinder: 1154 & 1155

Parking & Starting Point:
Parking is available at The Ridgeway Centre, Courthill (GR.394849). This is also the starting point of your ride.

Parking Note: The Ridgeway Centre at Courthill is close to the A338 Wantage to Hungerford road. It is a superior grade Youth Hostel with parking and stabling. The stabling is only suitable for smaller horses.

Route Description:

1.   From The Ridgeway Centre ride to the A338 and carefully cross over the road and onto a track. After one mile this track joins The Ridgeway. Continue to ride along The Ridgeway to GR.410841 and here, where there is a signpost for public right of way, fork right to ride over Lattin Down to the B4494 road (GR.420833).

2.   Cross over to the iron gate which lies to the right of the Lockinge Kiln Farm drive. Go into the pasture field and ride diagonally across to the next iron gate which has a waymark and, following the line of telegraph poles, take the track to Farnborough.

3.   When you reach a road (GR.430820), turn left and ride through Farnborough village and at the road

junction, follow the sign to West and East Ilsley. Take care round the 'S' bends when leaving the village. *The church on the right has a lovely stained glass window by John Piper, in memory of Sir John Betjeman, the former Poet Laureate; the Old Rectory on the left was used in the television series 'Trainer'.* At Upper Farm (GR.437820) turn right, keeping the water tank on stilts on the left. After a few yards you will see a waymarked bridleway.

4.   Follow this bridleway to a four-armed bridleway signpost (GR.451816). Turn right and ride until you reach the road (GR.453812). *Sometimes this track is wet.*

5.	On reaching the road, turn right. There is woodland on the left of the road and where this ends, turn left into the signposted bridleway. Follow the bridleway keeping the hedge on the right and where it turns to follow the road, ride straight on towards the woodland. Go through a gateway, which is usually open, and into an area of trees and onto a stony track. Turn left at the signposted 'Public Right of Way' and left again at the first bridleway sign (GR.459803). When you reach an area where there is woodland on both sides do not be tempted to leave the track to avoid puddles as there is also fallen wire on both sides. Ride downhill with Pines on the right and grassy area on the left, then ride across an area of open grass and straight on into a track where there is a woodland on the right and a field hedge on the left.

6.	At a T-junction of tracks, turn left into the signposted byway. Where the track forks take the left turning which is signposted 'Public Bridleway' - *sometimes the signpost is hard to see.* A few yards further on take the track to the right which is signposted 'Public Bridleway - Recreational Route', and at the chalky track turn right where the signpost reads 'Public Bridleway'. Go through the gateway to the left of a cattle grid with Hodcott House on the right and at the tarmac drive turn left.

7.	When you reach the public road by 'Old Chapel' at West Ilsley(GR.476824)*, turn right and then into the track on the left, signposted 'Cart Track and Recreational Route'. Where the track forks take the right-hand track and ride uphill. At the bridleway sign, 'Recreational Route', bear left and follow the ditch on the left. Ride between two white-painted posts and onto The Ridgeway (GR.487837).

8.	Turn left and at Bury Down Car Park, cross the Chilton to West Ilsley road. Ride towards the woodland on the horizon. At the woodland (GR.458850)**, turn left, signposted 'Public Right of Way'. The track follows the gallops on the left. At an iron gate leading onto the gallops, the track bears right between a fence and a hedge. Follow this track to the road (GR.452834).

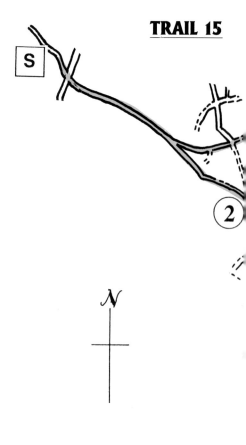

TRAIL 15

S

2

9.   On reaching the road, turn right and just before a house known as Land's End, turn right onto the signposted bridleway. A gravel track passes through the gateway. Ride to the left of the gateway along the turf track, then over cross tracks and uphill to The Ridgeway (GR.433846).

10.   Turn left along The Ridgeway and ride uphill past the Monument and then downhill to the B4494 road. Cross over the road and continue along The Ridgeway to GR.410841. From here retrace your outward ride back to The Ridgeway Centre and your parking place.

*It is possible to turn left here and ride through the village to The Harrow Public House which serves refreshments. On leaving, take the track to the right, just beyond The Harrow, this will take you to The Ridgeway where you turn left to continue your ride at GR.458850***

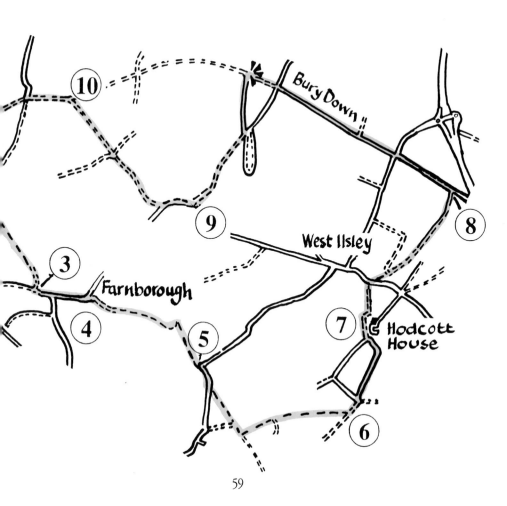

SOUTHDOWNS - RIDGEWAY LINK

TRAIL 16

A 20 MILE LINEAR ROUTE (SOUTH TO NORTH)

Ordnance Survey Maps:
Landranger: 174
Pathfinder: 1155, 1171, 1186 & 1187

Parking and starting point:
Parking is available for unloading your horse between Combe Gibbet and Walbury Hill, in the car park at the foot of Walbury Hill, above Upper Inkpen (GR.370620). *(It should be noted that the car park is rather isolated).* This is your starting point.

Parking Note: Although the Combe Gibbet road is steep, it is still feasible for a lorry to use it.

Of Interest:
The South Downs - Ridgeway Link runs from Cheriton on the South Downs Way in southern Hampshire. From Brown Candover in Hampshire it is an easily followed byway for most of its length. North of Basingstoke, at Hannington, it follows the crest of the north Wessex Downs with its glorious views. It is not easily accessible by road once it has passed the A34 south of Newbury, where it passes through a series of large private estates and is only breached by small narrow roads. This only makes the landscape on each side less spoilt.

Walbury Hill is the highest chalk hill in Britain being 297 metres high and it is worth riding across to the trig point to enjoy a total all round view of a truly splendid landscape. The trig point is 100 metres south of the starting point.

Route Description:

1.	From your parking place follow the track for 0.50 miles to meet the Inkpen to Faccombe road. Go east along this road for 0.25 miles and then turn left towards East Woodhay. Almost immediately turn left onto the waymarked Wayfarers Way again. *This section is muddy and rutted.* Take the next turn left down the hill onto a track which crosses the road and leads to Highwood Farm (GR.389624). *This is also the County Boundary for Hampshire and Berkshire.*

2.	Ride straight through the farm and down the concreted farm drive to meet a road (GR.392628). Here you turn left and then right going round a white house. Follow this road for 0.75 miles and when you come to a crossroads, turn left. *Ride carefully along this road; it can be slippery.* After 0.75 miles look for the byway on the right which is signposted Holly Lane and turn onto it. *This can be muddy at times but is usually pleasant riding - you may also see a herd of Fallow deer.* After a mile you will emerge on the corner of a road. Bear right and trot on up to Holtwood crossroads (GR.418642). Take the narrow lane to the left and ride along until you come to Hamstead crossroads. Go straight across here and up Park Lane which is very steep and narrow. *On the right is the boundary to Hamstead Park the former family seat of the Earls of Craven. From the top of the hill, just* before you reach the crossroads, if you look across the park you will see the 18th Century house, although the monumental gate piers and stretch of brick wall belong to a 17th Century mansion that was the size of Blenheim Palace. Unfortunately this was burnt down in the 17th Century before it had been occupied by Elizabeth of Bohemia who was the great love of the first Earl.

TRAIL 16.

3.   Turn right at the next crossroads with the Craven Estate buildings and gate piers on your right and ride down the hill. *Note the superb view of the Kennet Valley on your left. The Norman Hamstead Marshall Church, backed by the contemporary Motte and Bailey, overlook the river valley, the canal lock and the Great Western Railway line. The whole area has been strategic from the earliest times; even the pill-boxes from World War II still bear mute witness to this.* Once over all the 'transport systems', turn right past The Water Rat Public House at Marsh Benham (GR.426675)- *this is a good refreshment*

place - and continue down the lane to turn right keeping the railed paddocks of Benham Stud on your left. Ride up a slope with a good grass verge - *a suitable place to canter* - and in 0.50 miles you will meet the Bath Road (A4) (GR.432682). *This is a very busy road and must be CROSSED WITH CARE.*

4.   Ride straight over the road and up the right-handed road to the B4000 (Ermin Street), Newbury/Lambourn road at Stockcross. Ignore the 'No Entry' sign and go straight across into a lane with the village school on the right. After 0.25 miles there is a byway to the left, pass this and take the next byway on the left, which is a short deep track and somewhat muddy. You will emerge on to a tiny road. *Where the

61

lane meets the broken bridge, climb up the bank on the right of the lane and on to the disused railway track and make your way right-handed along the well surfaced track. This track ends in a small setaside field opposite the road to Bagnor.

If you do not wish to go onto the disused railway line you may continue along the lane to the Lambourn Valley road (GR.434691) but this is quite busy along this stretch, being narrow with no verge until it meets the turning to Bagnor.

5.   Take the road into Bagnor and bear right at The Blackbird Public House (GR.454692) to take the signposted byway up a narrow track between cottages and a golf course and make your way up to Snelsmore Common.

6.   Here, at the top of a steep bank which is at the end of the byway, you will find an all-weather horse track. Ride along this track and after approximately 100 yards take the signposted bridleway to enter into a car park area. Take the signposted track just to the left of the Park Attendants hut. This is a short stretch of all-weather track and takes the rider through Birch trees to meet a small metalled road. Cross over and take one of the many well used tracks which will take you to the Maple Ash Livery Yard,

signposted on Pebble Lane. *(If you find yourself approaching a main road, the entrance to Pebble Lane is marked by a red and white pole and can be seen quite easily!).*

7.   Enter the lane and ride past Bussock Hill House and on down this deeply banked and somewhat muddy track onto the Winterbourne road and turn right towards the Wantage road. *CARE - there is fast traffic along the Wantage road.* Ride under the motorway and take the first turn right up to North Heath.

TRAIL 16
(Continued)

8.   Turn hard right along the marked byway and go through the ford at Hazelhanger Farm and thence on to the Gidley Lane.   Ride along this lane crossing straight over at Woods Folly and into Old Street. *It is about one mile from entering Gidley Lane to the far end of Old Street.* Continue along this ancient signposted byway until it meets The Ridgeway at West Ginge Down**. *There is one muddy stretch of track lying north of Catmore, and 0.50 miles of marsh at the edge of Parkwood. Soon after you are on good fast going and then, after the road crossing at Lands End, you are rewarded with a lovely sweeping ride, and a gallop if you wish, up to The Ridgeway and all that lies beyond.*

** *If you mean to go east to join the Swans Way, after the next crossroads you must look out for a right fork, south-east of Stanmore, which branches off to East Ilsley. East Ilsley is full of pubs and has at least one useful livery yard with grazing, which would make a useful overnight stop.*

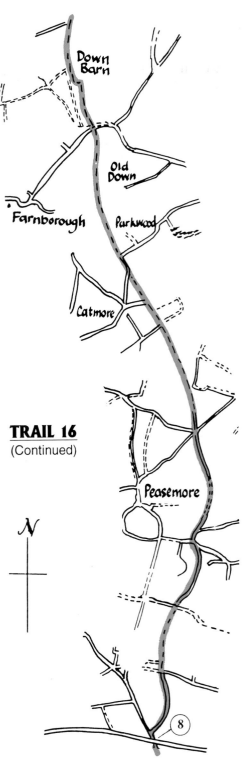

TRAIL 16
(Continued)

THE BRITISH HORSE SOCIETY

The British Horse Society was founded in 1947 when two separate equestrian bodies - The National Horse Association and the Institute of the Horse and Pony Club - decided to join forces and work together for the good of both horse and rider.

It is a marriage that has proved to be a great success and the British Horse Society has steadily increased its membership from just 4000 in the late 1960's to over 60,000 in the 1990's.

By becoming members of the British Horse Society, horse lovers know they are joining a body of people with a shared interest in the horse. Members can be sure that they are contributing to the work of an equine charity with a primary aim to improve the standards of care for horses and ponies. Welfare is not only about the rescuing of horses in distress (which we do); it is also about acting to prevent abuse in the first place. There are many means to achieving this: by teaching and advising, by looking to the horse's well-being and safety, by providing off-road riding, by encouraging high standards in all equestrian establishments, and fighting for the horse's case with government and in Europe.

The British Horse Society works tirelessly towards these aims thanks to the work of its officials at Stoneleigh and its army of dedicated volunteers out in the field.

Membership benefits the horse lover as well as the horse; the Society can offer something to all equestrians, whether they are weekend riders, interested spectators or keen competitors. The benefits include free Third Party Public Liability and Personal Accident insurance, free legal advice, free publications, reductions to British Horse Society events, special facilities at the major shows, and free advice and information on any equine query.

Largely financed by its membership subscriptions, the Society welcomes the support of all horse lovers. If you are thinking of joining the Society and would like to find out more about our work, please contact the Membership Department at the following address:

The British Horse Society
British Equestrian Centre
Stoneleigh Park
Kenilworth
Warwickshire
CV8 2LR
(Telephone: 0203 696697)
Registered Charity No. 210504